If the kindest souls were rewarded with the longest lives, dogs would out live all humans...

TALOOLA 2006 - 2020

A
DIY GUIDE
TO UNFUK YOUR HEAD

BRIAN GLENN
2020

CONTENTS

INTRODUCTION

If you are looking for someone to understand your predicament, your pain, your hurt, your past, then forget it.

The only person who is closest to understanding you is yourself.

Sometimes you can't see the wood for the trees and we just want someone to help us to get our life back together.

And whilst certain therapies can help to ease the pain and understand some things, friends and family can help too; but there is only so much they can do. In the long term, it really is all about you.

The good news is, you and you alone have the power to make your life better.

You my dear friend have a very important birth right...

It is your birth right to be happy.

This book will help you to reclaim your birth right to be happy by first taking control away from others and empowering yourself to become your own healer.

You must be fed up by now of telling your story, visiting therapists, and asking yourself 'why me?' only to gain temporary freedom from the pain and then return to that old vicious cycle of self-destruction.

This book comes from a lifetime of personal pain, twenty five years of helping people to help themselves and offers valid and tested solutions to your issues in ways that you have probably never considered before.

My personal journey has not been pain free, in fact it's only the past 10 years or so that I managed to make a difference, following many years in therapy, long stays in psychiatric wards and numerous visit to therapists, counsellors, psychologists and psychiatrists.

My break came when I finally made a conscious and determined decision to fuk them all off, grasp the nettle and set off on a journey of fixing myself.

My personal remit was to keep things simple, not dig too deep and shelve all the woo woo bollocks that people had fed me over the years.

I had nothing to lose, all the other 'traditional' stuff I had tried had clearly not worked. There was only me left!

I quickly discovered a way forward that also was painful, but the difference being that the pain was a one-off experience and short-lived. It was the beginning of my journey to happiness.

So from finding myself homeless twice in my life, one of which making my home under a cosy duvet in Woolworths shop doorway, to living the dream here in Sunny Spain, feeling happy for the first time in my life, with a successful and thriving business behind me, and an amazing partner supporting me, I would like to take this opportunity to share with you some of the life changing techniques I discovered along the way.

FOREWARD

The first time I actually met Brian was just over halfway through my Hypnotherapy training course which Brian had developed and nurtured over the years. We were all so excited when our tutor announced his imminent visit.

Prior to this visit, I had only heard about Brian via my tutor, who had shared some very positive, inspirational and funny stories about him and his life. I have to say myself and many other students had become very curious and interested to meet this character in the flesh.

From that first meeting, humour wise, Brian and I clicked and from that moment onwards, he has regularly had me howling with laughter, just like I did at school. At the time this was exactly what I needed.

As we continued to get to know each other more, Brian was also incredibly supportive in helping me get through some tough personal issues that were deeply affecting my happiness. His support and genuine care for my wellbeing was astounding, I soon realised that this person really genuinely cares about how people feel! As Brian states in this book

"it is your given birth-right to be happy"

Over time, as I grew as a Therapist, Brian offered me a position to retrain and join the tutoring team at Innervisions School of Clinical Hypnosis, where Brian is principal. I'll always be grateful that Brian was able to see passed the wounds that I had at that time and see the potential in me.

As we began working together, it became apparent that business wise we were from two vastly different worlds. My background was very corporate and Brian had never experienced any formal corporate training. Slowly disagreements and resentment, through communications issues began to rise, and over time an unspoken negative and uncomfortable atmosphere grew between us. It started to feel like we were enemies and no longer that duo that would be unable to breathe from laughing. Where was all that laugher now?

As things do, eventually it all came to ahead and we had a full-blown argument, at the time I was devastated and looking back I realised, so was Brian. Although it felt like the end of the world at that time, in hindsight it actually was the making of our working relationship and friendship!

With the air cleared and positive restructuring within Innervisions, we were able to move forward with a new understanding of how we worked. Since then we have gone from strength to strength, becoming firm friends and developing our own unique way of successfully working together. The laughter is back, with respect and appreciation, but also there is a real empathy of each other's individuality, interlaced with healthy and practical boundaries.

There is no holding back when it comes to Brian being Brian, he doesn't mince his words and also wears his heart on his sleeve. The integrity, support and guidance that he has repeatedly shown me personally and many, many others is vast. He is a straight talker and drops more 'F' bombs (and worse!) than I have ever encountered, but his compassion and kindness is what shines through. Especially for those who are ready to embrace it.

I have learnt many things from Brian that have increased my daily happiness and this book is filled with a treasure trove of life changing gems and pearls of wisdom that can do the same for you. The content maybe a slightly smaller number of pages than most books, but wow does it all pack a mind-blowing punch!

A favourite quote of mine in the book is:

"It's a bit like drinking poison and expecting someone else to die."

Understanding this simple metaphor helped heal me after a very toxic relationship and has since helped me let go of old hurts and wrong doings, from people throughout my life. It allowed me to understand the difference between forgiveness and not condoning bad behaviour.

Brian has a very interesting and colourful past, and he is always proud to share some of his darker times during his teenage years. A true and genuine example of how people can harness the power that is inherent in us all to create a better life for ourselves. Most of which are shared in the proceeding pages of this book.

As I read the book it gave me many lightbulb moments and deeper understandings that have instantly upgraded my mindset and given me further insight about who I am.

For me, this book is straight to the point, with a no nonsense therapy style that actually resonated, and went straight into my psyche and instantly upgraded it, and you too can experience an improved new normal way of living simply by taking the time to read his book.

I really don't think you will be the same person after reading this book!

Enjoy.

Charlotte x

NFINITE NUMBER OF YOU'S?

A different version of you exists in the minds of every person who knows you, or ever knew you.

During my darker days, my psychologist told me that I needed to find out who I am and what I am about... Sounded like a good idea at the time, so I had a go and all I did was confuse myself even more.

For ease of numbers, Imagine one hundred people know you. If you asked those hundred people to write a sentence about who they perceive you to be, then you would have one hundred different variations.

Those variations could be...

From

A complete lying, deceitful, arrogant asshole

To

A charming, intelligent, generous and loving person.

Furthermore, if you were to ask those 100 people the exact same question one year later, they would probably answer completely different. To the extent that the person who rated you as a charming, intelligent, generous and loving person, may now even describe you as a complete lying, deceitful, arrogant idiot, due to some incident during the past twelve months.

So not only do those hundred people have their own unique perception of who you are, their perception to who you are is changing on a second by second basis.

Now apply this to all the people who have ever known you since you were born, and all the people who you will meet from this day forward.

Now take into account your own perception of who you are, which is also changing on a second by second basis from the day you were born.

This gives an almost infinite number of perceptions as to who you are!

So who are you?

Well, in the simplest of terms, all we really are is a biological mass of constantly changing chemistry; changing on a second by second basis.

Differing perceptions

1. Mother's/Father's perception
2. Best friend's perception
3. Brother's/sister's perception
4. Work mates' perception

5. Doctor's perception
6. Bloke down the pub's perception
7. Son/daughter's perception
8. Your boss's perception
9. Acquaintances' perception
10. School teachers' perception
11. Your partner's perception
12. Your mentor's perception

Every single person who knows you or who ever met you has a different perception of you which is changing on a second by second basis.

Just try poking your best mate in the eye, calling them an insulting name and watch their perception of you change in an instant.

So who are you?

The answer can only be given accurately and honestly in this very moment. In this moment you are simply a biological mass of constantly changing chemistry. Even our thoughts have a significant effect on our biological and chemical makeup.

But here is something interesting...

The way you conduct your life is based on the sum of every thought you ever had and every decision that you ever made.

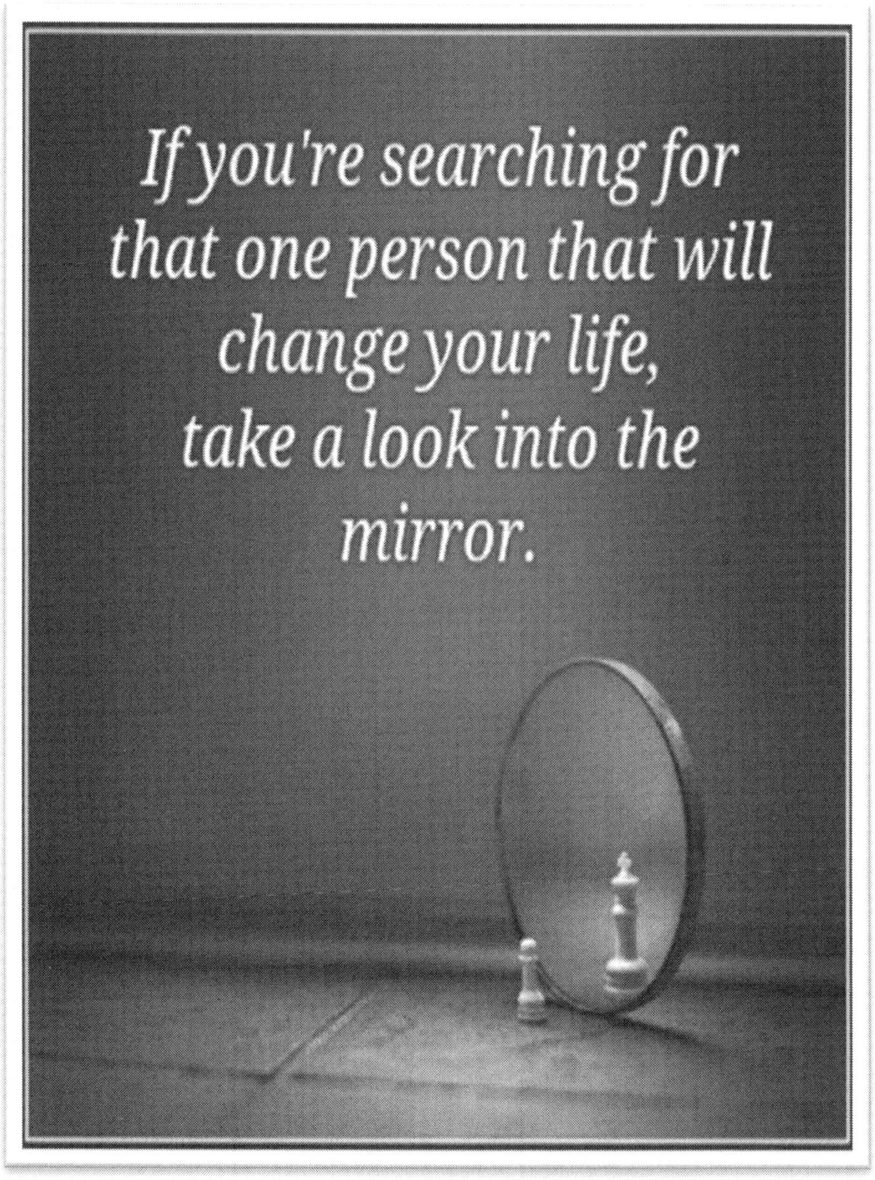

It is in those very moments when everything looks hopeless that we have a real chance to grow into something better: what the caterpillar calls the end of the world, we call a butterfly!

Who we are now is not who we were last year, last week, yesterday or even a minute ago. Life never stands still, no matter what we do. Change is the very nature of existence; our thoughts, feelings, beliefs, ideas, even our relationships are as changeable as rain and sunshine, or night and day.

But, as much as change is inevitable, it is not always welcome or easy to deal with. It can upset our world and generate many conflicting feelings.

However, it is in those very moments when everything looks hopeless that we have a real chance to grow into something better: what the caterpillar calls the end of the world, we call a butterfly!

The journey to such transformation is smoother when we can step back from anger, fear or grief and take a breath, before emotion takes over. Then we can enable the issue to pass, for not even those feelings that seem so enormous, important or overwhelming stay the same. Given time, what is vital to us now will soon lose its relevance.

Knowing this means that we can be more at ease with change. As thoughts come and go, as we watch emotions rise and fall like waves, as physical, emotional or mental pain is felt and then gone, we see how this coming and going applies to everything, even our breath. This sense of rhythm informs us that, if we wait long enough, even the darkest of times will also pass.

Mahatma Gandhi famously said, "You must be the change you want to see in the world." In other words, although life changes are inevitable, we can also initiate personal change so we can rise to the challenge and become a bigger and better person as a result. How do we do this? We believe the best ways are to recognize that change is inevitable, that there is always the potential for positive change in every moment and to stay grounded and in touch with our peace.

Everything is coming and going

Everything that is happening now will change into something else; every thought and feeling, no matter how intense or dramatic, will one day be immaterial. Without change in ourselves we become stifled and stagnant. As nothing lasts forever, we can appreciate every moment, fully and completely, knowing it will never happen again. Coming to a still place, gently breathe in and out, silently repeating:

"And this too shall pass."

Each day starts a new

We always have the opportunity to transform fear into courage, selfishness into kindness and loss into fresh beginnings, just as palm trees transform muddy rainwater into sweet coconut milk. Spring is here, with new life bursting forth, and in the same way we too are capable of creating a new life for ourselves in each and every moment.

For surely, life is about not having answers and taking chances, all without knowing what is going to happen next. Sitting quietly, breathing deeply and joyfully, silently repeat:

"I open my mind and heart to new possibilities."

Nobody can go back and start a new beginning, but anyone can start today and make a new ending.

Being peace

The clue to transformation is being able move with the waves, to paddle in the dip so we are ready to ride the next crest. Meditation creates a space where times of pain, sadness, anger, fear, hurt, confusion, doubt and all our other conflicting emotions can come and be known and gently released. It enables us to be present with whatever is and to accept, honour and move with change. All kinds of thoughts may arise, or feelings, sensations and images. We watch, without denying, pushing away or holding on. We can comfortably rest in stillness, without any judgment or discrimination.

Just as the breath comes in and out, so it is like the coming and going of all change.

Breathe in and out gently, and watch the natural rhythm of your breath. Silently repeat:

"May I be easeful, may I be peaceful, may I flow with the changes. And enjoy each moment, as it is a precious gift!"

Be the Change
you wish to see in the
World

YOUR THOUGHTS BECOME YOUR REALITY

Today, in this very moment, you have become the sum of every thought and every choice that you ever made.

Be careful what you think. Your brain is like a biological computer and will obey every single instruction that you give it.

Everything starts with a thought and manifests itself into your personal reality. For example buying this book started with a thought and now you physically have it. That job you had, that relationship you had, that holiday you went on, that cup of tea you just drank, ALL started with a thought and eventually manifested itself into your reality.

Ironically, all the thoughts you are having today, are probably exactly the same, or very similar to the thoughts you were having weeks ago, or even months and years ago. So it does indeed make sense to me that you are manifesting the same shit into your life as you were all that time ago!

There is no change without change.

If you always do what you have always done, you will always get what you always got. If you want something different, do something different, and it all starts with a simple thought!

Thoughts become things, choose the good ones...

WE ARE ALL THE SAME, BUT DIFFERENT

Every man on the planet and every woman on the planet are identical. Think about it, if you are a man, and you place all your bodily organs in a pile on the floor, and every other man on the planet did the same, we would never know whose was whose, they would all look identical. We all have the same kit, heart, lungs, liver, kidneys, spleen, brain etc.

So the one single and amazing thing that actually makes us all different, is the way that we think! – And whatever we think, becomes our personal reality.

A rich person 'thinks' differently to a poor person.
A poorly person 'thinks' differently to a well person.
A good golfer 'thinks' differently to a bad golfer.
A confident person 'thinks' differently to an insecure person.
A car mechanic 'thinks' differently to a policeman.
A hairdresser 'thinks' differently to a chef.
A good person 'thinks' differently to a bad person.

So...

If you want to be a millionaire, THINK like a millionaire.
If you want to be happy, THINK like a happy person.
If you want to be healthy, THINK like a healthy person.
If you want to be a hairdresser, THINK like a hairdresser.
If you want to be a golfer, THINK like a golfer.

The other interesting thing about us humans is that we all believe that we are right! But if we were ALL right, we would ALL be completely identical. Rich, happy, sad, miserable, healthy, poorly…

So, if you believe that it's going to be hard to change the way you think, you are absolutely right. Conversely, if you believe it is going to be easy to change the way that you think, you are also right.

So, from now on, you must BELIEVE that changing the way that you think is going to be easy! – Very easy.

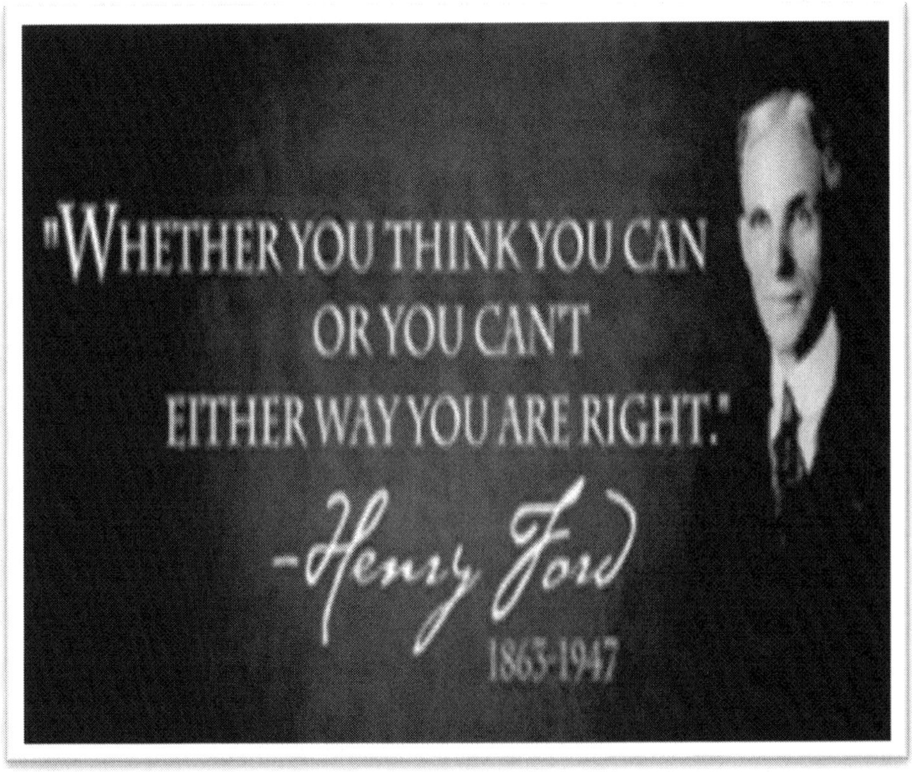

ACCOUNTABILITY

Some of us had pretty shit childhoods. Please be aware that what happened when you were a child was not your fault. You had very little or no control over what happened to you as a child. But the good news is, now that you are an adult, you do have control over your life in the now.

There is no future in the past. Your past only exists in your head, but your future is now in your hands.

The only thing you can change about the past, is how you let it affect you now.

The following page is vital – it's your first step to recovery.

In my 25 years' experience as a therapist, and based on my own personal experiences, I cannot emphasise how important this first step towards your complete recovery is.

Either close this book now and throw it in the bin, or take on board carefully what I am about to share with you regarding your complete recovery.

STEP ONE: NO MORE FINGER POINTING

This is your first and most important step.

Stop pointing fingers. Did you notice, that when you point your finger at someone or something, there are **THREE** fingers pointing back at you. Go ahead, try it.

Stop blaming your temper, alcohol issues, bad behaviour, sadness, badness, anxiety, depression, panic attacks, obesity etc. on other people or events.

DID YOU KNOW...

The person you hate, is actually loved by lots of people
The job you hate, some people love
The town you live in is actually a nice place
The person you hate, you probably once loved

The job you hate, you probably once loved
The person you married was what YOU chose to do
The house you live in was your choice.

The car you drive is the car you once longed for.

The route you drove to work that day was your choice.

In reality, there is nothing wrong with that house, that job, that person, that car etc. It's your personal perception to that house, that job, that person, that car etc. that's the real problem. And the good news is... you can change your perception.

As an adult **YOU** are responsible for **ALL** your actions. Own the choices you made in the past and if you are not happy about your life in the now, **CHANGE IT!** It's your responsivity.

The person that hurt you in the past, is just that, in the past. Although they had some form of control over you then, they certainly don't have any control over you in the now. Unless of course you give them control.

So in the now, in this very moment in time, YOU have the control. You can be angry, bitter, annoyed, and even livid. All emotions that will affect your physical body in the now, and the person that hurt you is no longer around. In some cases dead! – But hey, are they still controlling you?

GRRR... That bastard did this to me
GRRR... I hate him/her

GRRR… I can't stand him/her

Saying all this with anger in your heart will only create life inhibiting chemicals in your body leading to low immune system, illness and disease. And guess what… the person you are angry towards is no longer in your life, maybe even dead. And if the person is alive, your anger and emotions won't affect him or her anyway. They don't give a shit about how you feel. The only person who it will affect in the long term is YOU.

Notice your blood pressure rise and your body react as you continuously take yourself into that destructive zone. Your immune system is compromised and your organs take a hit.

It's a bit like drinking poison and expecting someone else to die.

So here's the trick… do the opposite, send loving forgiving and compassionate thoughts and the same rules apply. The person you are sending these nice thoughts to is no longer in your life, maybe even dead. And if the person is alive, your nice thoughts won't affect him or her anyway. The only person who it will affect in the long term is YOU. So you start to feel good! Your body relaxes, your immune system strengthens and your organs are nourished.

NEUROPLASTICITY

Our brains are constantly being shaped by experience. Most of us have very different behaviours and thoughts today than we did 20 years ago. This shift is neuroplasticity in action; changes in brain structure and organisation as we experience, learn, and adapt.

With every repetition of a thought or emotion, we reinforce a neural pathway - and with each new thought, we begin to create a new way of being. These small changes, frequently enough repeated, lead to changes in how our brains work.

Neuroplasticity is the 'muscle building' part of the brain; the things we do, often we become stronger at, and what we don't use fades away. That is the physical basis of why making a thought or action over and over again increases its power. Over time, it becomes automatic; a part of us. We literally become what we think and do.

Neuroplasticity is at work throughout life, irrespective of age. Connections within the brain are constantly becoming stronger or weaker, depending on what is being used.

This ties in nicely with step two…

STEP TWO: NO MORE TALKING THERAPY

If I was to ask you to tell me something that you did yesterday, in order to explain it to me, you would have to relive it.

With this in mind, every time you tell your shit story about your childhood, your abusive ex, your tales of woe etc. you are actually reliving them. And every time you tell your story, you are in fact exercising the associated neural pathways in your brain that's associated with your story. Each time making the neural pathways stronger; thus keeping the story fresh in your mind and prohibiting you from moving on.

Some time ago, it was common practice for therapists to advise their clients to write down their negative thoughts in a journal. In hindsight, it's not really a good idea because as you are writing it down, you will also be re-experiencing them, and again exercising those associated neural pathways.

Here's the good news, the same thing happens when you share happy memories, stories and experiences. Also, if you can write these stories down it's a great way to exercise those associated happy neural pathways.

Try it, it may just work and the stuff you have been doing in the past has clearly not worked!

STEP THREE: ASSESSMENT

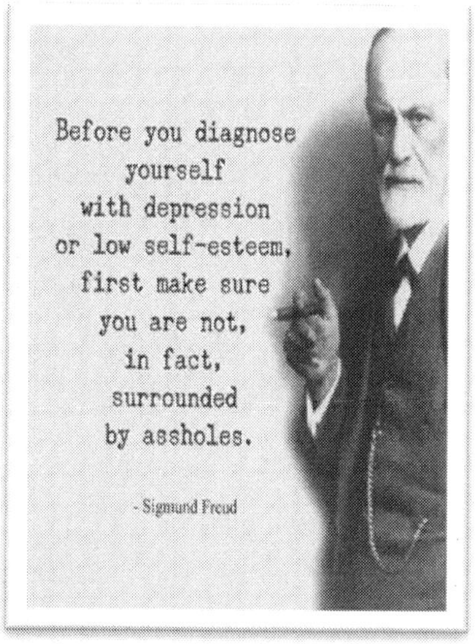

Take some time to assess the people that you allow to be part of your life. But do this by asking yourself 'is this person ***worthy*** of being a part of my life'

Start by writing a list of names on a sheet of paper, then write at the side of each name any positive gains they bring to your life.

Be clear on the fact that there is no person on this earth who has a right to treat you bad, unkind, or pull you down, or destroy your self-confidence.

Just because your mother is your mother does not give her the right to...

Just because your son is your son does not give him the right to...

Just because your husband is your husband does not give him the right to...

Poisonous people are all around us but chances are you're looking at the wrong people without realising it. They can sometimes be the most unexpected people and coming to terms with that is important.

Just because they've been in your life for a long time does not mean they aren't doing damage. Even the most important people in our lives can sometimes have the worst intentions, as sad as that is to realise.

Sometimes these people disguise themselves well and while they appear to be friends, they're actually your worst enemies and all the while you're completely oblivious.

Whether you use the word toxic, poisonous, or just dangerous overall, these people are not the kind of people you want in your life. They do nothing but drag you down and use your own words and actions against you.

There is nothing wrong with cutting ties with the people who are bringing you down and doing harm in your life, regardless of who those people are to you. Sometimes family can be harmful to us and in many cases leaving them in the past is a great way to promote a positive future. While cutting out family members and friends is a lot harder than letting go of strangers, if they're poisonous people they don't deserve to be in your life. They are simply not worthy of you.

You should never let someone who is constantly lying to you, blaming you for things you have no control over, and manipulating you into doing what they want to remain by your side. That only adds more fuel to the fire that is already raging and is a horrible idea. The only way to move on from that kind of thing is to remove that person, even if it hurts.

Just because they're your cousin, aunt, mom, or just your best friend doesn't mean that you owe them anything.

Just because they're your cousin, aunt, mom, or just your best friend doesn't give them a right to treat you like shit. You have choices. This is YOUR life. I know what you are thinking; you are thinking that if you dump all your family and friends based on what you just read, you would have no one there to support you. Well I am not suggesting that you line them all up and shoot them (metaphorically speaking). What I am suggesting is you make the decision to leave them behind and move on. And very soon you will find yourself attracting the right people into your life, who will be genuinely supportive.

And if you find that one of your new friends do not fit into your life for the right reasons, dump them too. You will be amazed how quickly new and like-minded people are attracted to you.

INTENTIONS

Throughout life, it is inevitable that people are going to hurt you. The trick here is to ask yourself a simple question.

"did the person deliberately intend to hurt me"

If the answer is "yes", Fek em off. If the answer is "no" consider forgiving them. It's all about intentions.

STEP FOUR: GET REAL

Oh we do fool ourselves with stupid and nonsensical phrases.

Here are some things I have often heard people say…

"I would live in a garden shed with the right person"

Yup, for about 4 days. The first two days you would shag each other senseless, the third day you would feel bored and the fourth day you would be running home to see who's posted on your Facebook wall.

"I am non-materialistic"

Yeah right, send me your car keys, your watch, your mobile phone, your TV, that nice necklace… I don't think so. When I hear people say this, what I really hear is the person telling me that they don't feel worthy of all the nice things that life has to offer. Or they are justifying why they have nothing.

Hey, I'll tell you what, I've been homeless twice in my life, one of which my home was Woolworths shop doorway with absolutely nothing. Not even hope. And now I have lots of nice things in my life and I know the difference.

Program your mind to believe that it is ok to have nice things, and you are worthy of having money, nice things, possessions etc. Okay, I hear you and you are right, you can't take them to your grave with you, but you can enjoy them whilst you are alive.

'I just want someone to make me happy'

Oh dear, did you not realise that if you empower a person to make you happy, you are also empowering them to make you sad too? You are giving away control. Also, what a burden to put on a loved one. Expecting them to always keep you happy. That's not love, that's control.

Happiness is your responsibility, not anyone else's. More on this later.

'I don't want to appear selfish'

Well, whether you like it or not, one of the main survival mechanisms that all human beings is being selfish. And trying to be unselfish just leads to misery and anxiety. I want you to understand that it ok and perfectly normal to be selfish. When other people call you selfish it's usually because you are doing things for yourself and not for them!

So one of the things I would like you to allow yourself to be is…. **BE SELFISH** at least until your sort your life out.

*'I **can't survive without???'***

Oh you will, you are hardwired to survive. I know this from my time living in Woolworths' shop doorway. One of your most powerful and basic instincts is to survive. All you need is courage and the right people around you to support you.

So come on, stop fooling yourself with unfounded and life inhibiting statements.

'I just want someone to love me unconditionally'

Well, I am sorry, but you are never going to find love. The fact of the matter is, the more you love someone, the more conditions there are. Some of the conditions may be things associated with violence, domestic abuse, fidelity etc.

If you want unconditional love, get yourself a dog.

If you locked your partner and your dog in the boot of your car and left them for an hour, see who would be glad to see you on your return.

'I will never be happy'

Well. You are absolutely right this time. Repeating this affirmation on a regular basis will ensure its validity.

STEP FIVE: CLOSURE

Closure is a very important part of self-healing and also an essential ingredient to maintain your future mental health.

Everything you do is based on you making choices on stimulating your senses. Dopamine, the chemical responsible for happy feelings.

Remember how you once felt when you first met the man you now hate, you were full of loving emotions and fuelled with a high amount of dopamine. Then after a period of time, those feelings change and turn to anger and resentment. This is not good from a subconscious perspective. It causes confusions and grief.

This is a form of grieving.

The exact same thing happens when we don't put closure on minor things, like throwing a pair of shoes in the bin after they are worn out. When you bought them, you bought them because you liked them they gave you a nice feeling and a dopamine rush. But now you are throwing them away. Again, this is also not good from a subconscious perspective. It also causes confusions and grief.

So my advice here is to always spend a minute or two with a personal 'closure' ritual so that you are able to move on to new and exciting things. (A new pair of shoes perhaps ;-))

Close your eyes, and just imagine those shoes walking away from you into the distance… Simple eh.

Close your eyes and imagine saying goodbye to your ex and wishing them well. Imagine him/her walking shamefully over the mountain.

Do it your way! – But make a habit of doing it regularly, especially when things come to an end.

STEP SIX: DISCOVER YOUR LIFE'S PURPOSE

We all need a purpose. If we don't attempt to consciously find a reasonably rewarding life purpose, our subconscious will often find one for us. This can often be a negative purpose like drugs, excess drinking, self-harm, eating disorder, etc.

Your life purpose could be to enjoy a good job and earn a good living. Maybe your life purpose could be to help others, or to manufacture the best curtains in the country.

It's a personal thing. One of the best ways to find your purpose is to isolate yourself in a place that's beautiful. Maybe by the sea or in the countryside. Alone, with a notebook and plenty of time to enjoy freedom, solitude and peace. Set your intentions in your mind before you go.

The way I discovered my life's purpose was back in 1991, whilst in a regular meditative state I simply asked myself 'what is my life purpose?' I was so disappointed when the answer never came. But to my surprise, three nights later, I woke in the early hours with the proposition that my personal life's purpose was to help a million people during my lifetime.

Of course I accepted that proposition and continue on my quest to help a million people.

Maybe you will become part of my million now that you are reading my book!

STEP SEVEN: GRATITUDE

Gratitude, or appreciation for the good things that happen in life, is an essential part of building happiness. When you're going through a tough time it can be hard to remember to be grateful for the good stuff, but there are a stack of benefits that can be gained from working gratitude into your everyday life. Find out more about ways to increase your gratitude and your awareness of things you can be grateful for.

This can help if:

- You want a strategy for helping to deal with a tough time
- You want to boost your mood
- You want to cultivate awareness and appreciation for the good things in your life.

What is gratitude?

Everyone has times when they feel aware of being thankful for a person or a situation. These moments give us a good feeling that we call 'gratitude'.

Feeling grateful just happens sometimes, but you can also make a special effort to increase how often you feel it. Research has shown that people with high levels of gratitude experience a whole bunch of benefits, so it's a great idea to increase your own.

The benefits of gratitude

Increasing your gratitude is useful because:

- It's an instant mood booster and feels great in the moment
- You're likely to feel closer to friends and family
- You're likely to enjoy your life more
- It's good for your physical health
- It's easier to cope with tough times
- Good things in life don't stick in our heads as easily as bad events.

This last point is really important. We tend to remember when bad things happen, and the time we spend thinking about them makes us unhappy. But, if we make an effort to increase how often we experience gratitude, it can balance out some of the negative stuff.

That doesn't mean that you should ignore/forget your problems, or that the things wrong with your life are unimportant. It just means that good memories will also stick in your mind, so you get to enjoy them for longer.

How to practise gratitude

Experiencing more gratitude is easy and doesn't take much time. Try these ideas and see what works best for you:

- Keep a gratitude journal. Take five minutes each day or once a week to think of and write down three things that have happened to you since the previous day or week that you're glad you experienced.

- Take pictures. Set yourself a mission to photograph little things in your everyday life that make you smile.

- Tell someone you're grateful to have them in your life. Whether it's someone you look up to, or someone who just makes you happy, take the time to tell them you're glad they're around.

You don't have to think up a whole bunch of really significant things in order to be grateful. You can be grateful for the smallest things, such as the sunshine, your morning coffee, or the fact that you made it to your train on time.

What can I do now?

Grab a notebook and start a gratitude journal.

Tell someone when you appreciate something that they've done.

ATTACHMENT

Be mindful of the fact that all your issues, problems, illnesses, aches and pains have not defined you as a person over the years. Sometimes all these things become an asset to us. We even surround ourselves with other people with similar issues and problems as ours even become competitive with it.

Buddhist people believe that the route of all pain is attachment.

If you find yourself in this situation, there are a number of things you can start to do to release yourself from that old definition of you.

Avoid sentences like:

- My depression
- My anxiety
- My IBS
- My nerves

Maybe replace them with

- The depression
- The anxiety
- The IBS
- The nerves

ANXIETY

Most people who suffer from anxiety, are probably living in the future, worrying and driving themselves crazy about stuff that has never even happened.

Worrying is like praying for something bad to happen.

Here I would like to share with you a fantastic technique for reducing your anxiety level. This procedure is adapted from a technique called EFT (Emotional Freedom Technique)

TAPPING

The basic sequence is straightforward and generally takes only a few minutes to learn. With a little practice, you will be performing each round in under a minute.

NOTE: While it is important to tap the correct area, you need not worry about being absolutely precise, as tapping the general area is sufficient.

IT'S ALL IN THE FINGERTIPS

The first thing to understand is that you will be tapping with your fingers. There are a number of acupuncture meridians on your fingertips, and when you tap with your fingertips you are also likely to be using not only the meridians you are tapping on but also the ones on your fingers.

Tap using the fingertips of your index finger and middle finger and with only one hand. Either hand works just as well.

Ideally, you will want to use your fingertips, not your finger pads as they have more meridian points. However, if you are a woman with long fingernails you should of course, use your finger pads (otherwise you may end up stabbing yourself).

You should also remove your watch and bracelets, as these would interfere with your use of the wrist meridian tapping.

TAP SOLIDLY - BUT DON'T HURT YOURSELF!

You should tap solidly, but never so hard as to hurt or bruise yourself.

When you tap on the points outlined below, you will tap around 5-7 times. The actual number is not critical, but ideally should be about the length of time it takes for one full breath. There is a distinct benefit for tapping through one complete respiratory cycle.

TAPPING STATEMENTS

As you are using the tapping sequence 1 to 5 in the following picture, continue to say out aloud a verbal statement that corresponds to your issue.

Here are some examples of verbal statements.

- "this horrible feeling"
- "this anxiety"
- "this pain"
- "this red wine"
- "this pork pie"
- "this craving for cheese"
- "this craving for chocolate"
- "this pain in my back"
- "this negative emotion"

So, go ahead and make your own verbal statement now which corresponds to your issue.

THE PROCEDURE

5 to 7 taps on all 5 points whilst at the same time repeating your issue.

Repeat procedure five times.

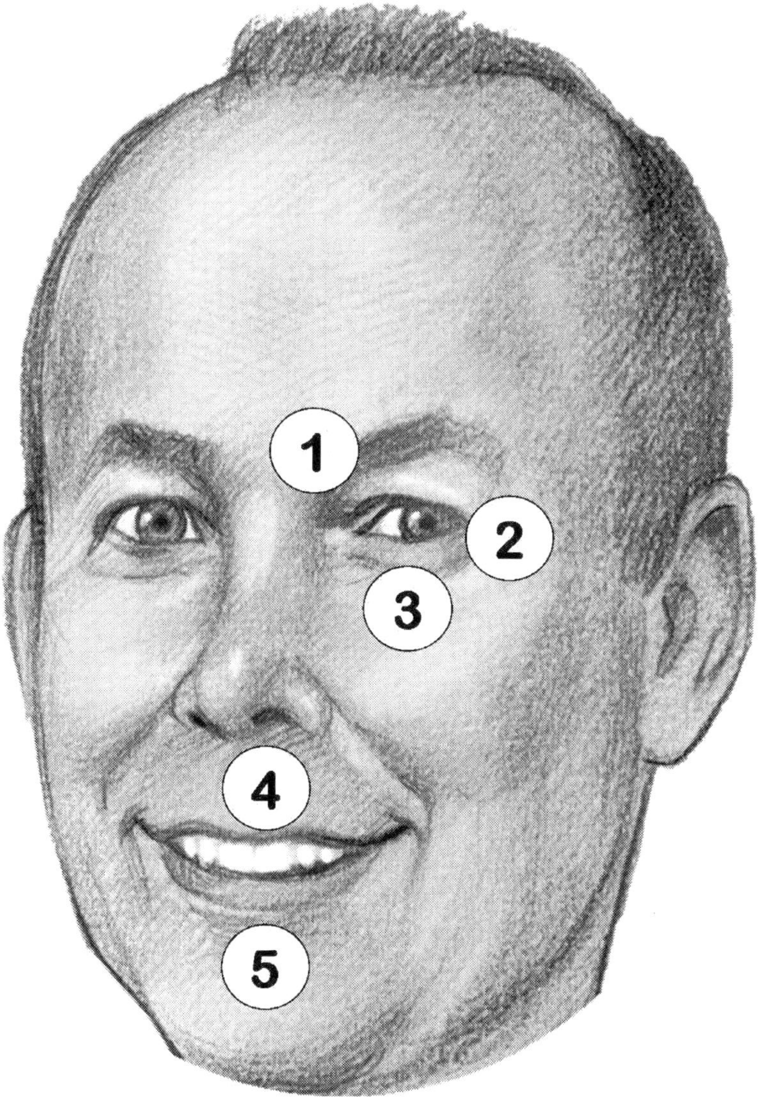

We now finish off the procedure by carrying out the following brainwave protocol.

1. With your head facing forward, move your eyes hard down to the left. (hold for 1 second)
2. With your head facing forward, move your eyes hard down to the right. (hold for 1 second)
3. With your head facing forward, roll your eyes in a circle clockwise.
4. With your head facing forward, roll your eyes in a circle anti clockwise.
5. Now hum happy birthday to you.
6. Count from one to five.

Repeat this procedure three times

The above sequence engages various brainwave patterns as the sequence continues. Humming 'happy birthday to you' engages the right brain (creative side) and counting from one to five engages the left brain (analytical side). Please note that the tune you hum does not have to be 'happy birthday to you', it's just that everyone knows that tune! You could actually hum your favourite tune instead if you choose to.

Further reading: Emotional Freedom Technique by Brian Glenn available from Amazon.

NUTRITION

You know, sometimes when you feel sad, fed up, down, depressed, miserable etc. it's nothing to do with 'life's hurdles' it could be something you keep eating that's messing with your 'happy' hormones.

In the past I avoided this subject like the plague. My ego kept telling me not to listen to people advising me on what I should and should not be eating. It's just made me want to eat more of 'my food'. I enjoyed the odd pork pie, a good steak, warm sausage roll and the good old traditional breakfast special. In hindsight, my ego almost killed me...

Just before my 60th birthday I had a bit of a health shock when I could not get out of the chair. I was drained of all energy and I honestly thought I was dying. I consulted a Kinesiologist who conducted various allergy tests on me. And yes, you got it, she told me I had poisoned my body by eating the food I loved. Almost everything I ate was closing down my body organs. I spent seventy five quid on that session and after it I felt like shit.

It soon became apparent to me that maybe I should listen to my Kinesiologist and at least see if I can get some value out of the experience, so I decided to give it a go. Plus the fact that I just spent seventy five quid!

One of the things that got in my way was that that I did not want to become one of those annoying vegetarian preachers having a go at everyone who eats meat.

Anyway, I invested in a top of the range fruit juicer, an orange juicer (we have lots of orange groves here in Spain) and loads of fruit and veg.

I never usually eat any fruit and veg, but I did not want to feel like shit anymore, so worth a go…

Anyway, within days I started to feel better. I went plant based and to my shock and surprise, after a week or two I started to like that food. I also stopped craving the shit food I had been accustomed to!

I certainly don't consider myself to be a full on veggie, I still treat myself to the odd breakfast special but cutting down on meat and processed food has certainly made a difference to my physical and mental wellbeing. I am not sure I will ever become a full time self-proclaimed vegetarian because to me it's more about balance.

Also, bear in mind (without me harping on too much) that some of the chemicals in some of the food you are eating could have a massive impact on your mental health! – Do some research yourself but keep it simple.

You would probably not put crap fuel into your car. And you probably feed you dog or cat 'proper' dog or cat food.

Your body is amazing, it knows exactly what you need; all you have to do is listen. It works fine providing that you take care of it and don't compromise your immune system or your mental wellbeing by eating shit!

AFFIRMATIONS

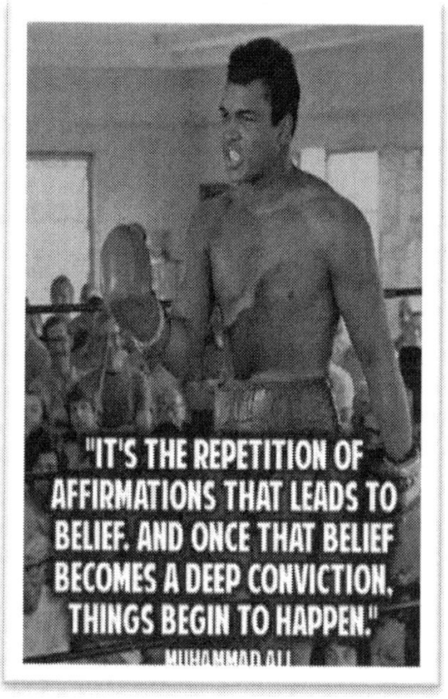

Be careful what you think. Your brain is like a biological computer and will obey every single instruction that you give it.

Affirmations connected with self can be written in large capitals and placed in strategic places around the home. Finding the words "I am assertive", written behind the toilet door often works wonders.

RULES OF AFFIRMATION

1. Affirmations must always be stated in the “NOW”

2. Use your own language patterns – even if you swear lots!

3. Use your own words

4. Keep sentences short and to the point

EXAMPLES OF GOOD AND BAD AFFIRMATIONS

BAD: "I am going to lose weight"
GOOD: "I am now slim and healthy"

BAD: "I am learning to like myself"
GOOD: "I now accept myself fully and completely"

BAD: "I am becoming stronger and fitter"
GOOD: "I am now fit and healthy"

BAD: "I want a job that I like"
GOOD: "I now enjoy my ideal job"

BAD: "I am getting better"
GOOD: "Every day I feel better and better"

BAD: "Tomorrow will be better"
GOOD: "Today I feel much better"

BAD: "I want to be wealthy"
GOOD: "I am now a wealthy person"

You don't need to believe the affirmations you are saying. Just say them with conviction. After all, those negative affirmations that you have been using for years are also untrue, but they still worked. Think about it!

A few years ago, I smiled when one of my hypnotherapy students proclaimed "oh those affirmations are rubbish, they never ever work". Of course he was right, but also it was evidence that they do indeed work!

MINDFULNESS

Many moons ago when I trained to be a clinical hypnotherapist, I realised that the main cause of environmental depression was the fact that some people were living primarily in their past. Conversely, the main cause of anxiety is people living in their future.

Here is one of my favourite phrases…

"Throughout my life, I have been through some terrible things…

…Some of which actually happened"

In my early years as a hypnotherapist I used to get people to focus more on the NOW – after all, it's really the only thing we have. And it's the most powerful point of power!

There's no future in the past…

In more recent times, I became excited when I learned the 'living in the now' concept that I had been using for years, is now recognised as a valid therapeutic method. This method is called 'mindfulness'.

RESEARCH

Overwhelming Mindfulness Research evidence shows that mindfulness boosts the immune system, intelligence, positive emotional states, self-awareness, creativity, happiness, compassion and more...

Rather than worrying about what has happened or might happen, when our clients are 'present' (or mindful), they can start to deal with whatever is happening. As clients become more skilled at managing their state of mind and emotional states, they gain resilience. Then, they are empowered to use their minds effectively instead of their minds running them ragged!

People start to see things as they really are (instead of how they imagine them to be through the filter of their story and habitual patterns), so can respond effectively and appreciate more fully.

When people are mindful, they stay with themselves and their experience as it unfolds, moment by moment. And this awareness has the quality of kindness, curiosity, openness and acceptance. Perceiving with all of the senses (sounds around, the touch of the air on our face, the taste in their mouth) takes their attention out of the stream of thinking. Clients open up to recognise that they are more than their thoughts or feelings.

Mindfulness is always available, every single moment; we just have to remember. Breaking the habit of being engrossed and fully identified with 'thought and thinking' and coming into awareness takes practice. Clients need to give the mind a focus, something to pay attention to.

Here are some simple practices that you can integrate into everyday life to help develop mindfulness.

Three mindful breaths – anytime – anyplace – anywhere

By giving all of our attention to the breath we can become calm and still the mind. The breath is always with us, but mostly we don't notice it. By purposely, moving our attention to our breath we come into the present moment, re-connect with ourselves and start afresh.

Notice how your body feels – anytime – anyplace – anywhere

Can you feel your hands? The air against your face? Get a sense of your feet on the floor. Purposefully, notice how your body feels from the inside. Move your focus of attention to different parts of your body. Your body is always present in the here and now.

Choose one routine activity that you will do mindfully. It may be washing your hands or walking to the bathroom or drinking a cup of tea. It can even be sitting at traffic lights. But, make a decision to choose one activity that you will REMEMBER to wake up for and do it consciously. Be aware of sense perceptions, sights/sounds/touch/smell/taste...

FACT:

Did you know, that it is physically and mentally impossible to be in an anxiety state at the same time as focusing on your vision, hearing, feelings, smell or taste at the same time! – So it is relatively easy for you to instantly suspend any anxiety state by focusing on any one of your five sensors.

Consequently, with regular practice, the frequency of anxiety states are greatly reduced and you regain full control.

Mindfulness is our capacity to be aware, right here, right now. We all have this ability naturally.

Look at a child playing and see how attentive they are; how curious, enraptured, fully engaging in the present moment. As we get older, our tendency is to develop the habit of getting 'lost' in the stories in our head, ruminating about the past / planning for the future.

This continuous stream of thinking that we are totally identified with and believe to be 'real' makes us overlook and disregard the endless possibility and power of the present moment.

It is also exhausting as we are continuously been driven unconsciously, by the 'to do list' and the thoughts about 'what I must get done today'.

INTRUSIVE THOUGHTS

Most people suffer at some time from intrusive negative thoughts. One brilliant way to distract from these intrusive thoughts is to focus on any of our sensors (vision, hearing, smells, taste or feelings). It's impossible to listen to those intrusive thoughts and focus consciously on one of our sensors at the same time. With practice the intrusive thoughts take second precedence.

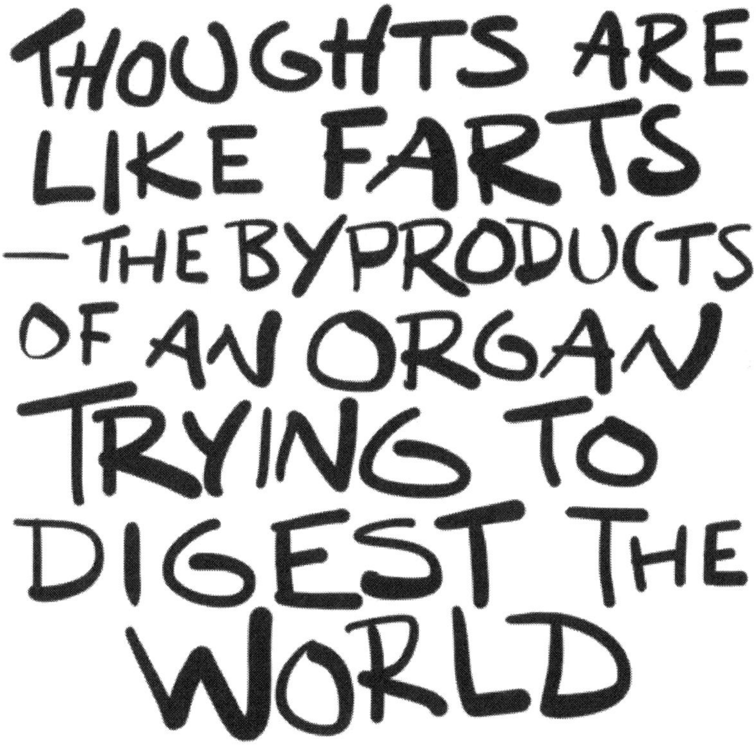

FURTHER READING: Mindfulness for the Frazzled by Ruby Wax

THE 90/10 PRINCIPLE

What is this principle?

10% of life is made up of what happens to you. 90% of life is decided by how you react.

What does this mean?

We really have no control over 10% of what happens to us. We cannot stop the car from breaking down. The plane will be late arriving, which throws our whole schedule off. A driver may cut us up in traffic. We have no control over this 10%. The other 90% is different.

You determine the other 90%.

How? By your reaction. You cannot control a red light, but you can control your reaction. Don't let people fool you; YOU can control how you react.

Let's use an example. You are eating breakfast with your family. Your daughter knocks over a cup of coffee onto your business shirt. You have no control over what just what happened. What happens next will be determined by how you react. You curse. You harshly scold your daughter for knocking the cup over.

She breaks down in tears. After scolding her, you turn to your spouse and criticize her for placing the cup too close to the edge of the table. A short verbal battle follows. You storm upstairs and change your shirt. Back downstairs, you find your daughter has been too busy crying to finish breakfast and get ready for school. She misses the bus. Your spouse must leave immediately for work.

You rush to the car and drive your daughter to school. Because you are late, you drive 40 miles an hour in a 30 mph speed limit. After a 15-minute delay and throwing £60 traffic fine away, you arrive at school. Your daughter runs into the building without saying goodbye. After arriving at the office 20 minutes late, you find you forgot your briefcase. Your day has started terribly. As it continues, it seems to get worse and worse. You look forward to coming home. When you arrive home, you find small problems in your relationship with your spouse and daughter.

Why? Because of how you reacted in the morning. Why did you have a bad day?

A. Did the coffee cause it?
B. Did your daughter cause it?
C. Did the policeman cause it?
D. Did you cause it?

The answer is "D".

You had no control over what happened with the coffee. How you reacted in those 5 seconds is what caused your bad day. Here is what could have and should have happened.

Coffee splashes over you. Your daughter is about to cry. You gently say, "It's ok honey, you just need to be a bit more careful next time". Grabbing a towel you rush upstairs. After grabbing a new shirt and your briefcase, you come back down in time to look through the window and see your child getting on the bus. She turns and waves. You arrive 5 minutes early and cheerfully greet the staff. Your boss comments on how good a day you are having.

Notice the difference? Two different scenarios. Both started the same. Both ended differently.

Why? Because of how you REACTED. You really do not have any control over 10% of what happens. The other 90% was determined by your reaction.

Here are some ways to apply the 90/10 principle. If someone says something negative about you, don't be a sponge. Let the attack roll off like water on glass. You don't have to let the negative comment affect you! React properly and it will not ruin your day. A wrong reaction could result in losing a friend, being fired, getting stressed out etc.

How do you react if someone cuts you up in traffic? Do you lose your temper? Pound on the steering wheel? Do you curse? Does your blood pressure skyrocket? Do you try and bump them? WHO CARES if you arrive ten seconds later at work? Why let the cars ruin your drive? Remember the 90/10 principle, and do not worry about it.

You are told you lost your job. Why lose sleep and get irritated? It will work out. Use your worrying, energy and time into finding another job. The plane is late; it is going to mangle your schedule for the day. Why take out your frustration on the flight attendant? She has no control over what is going on. Use your time to study, get to know the other passenger. Why get stressed out? It will just make things worse. Now you know the 90/10 principle. Apply it and you will be amazed at the results. You will lose nothing if you try it.

The 90/10 principle is incredible. Very few know and apply this principle.

The result?

Millions of people are suffering from undeserved stress, trials, problems and heartache. We all must understand and apply the 90/10 principle.

WRITE A LETTER

Sometimes, it's far easier for us to help our friends and family than it is to help our self. We seem to be able to offer great advice and express empathy to others but not to our self.

This is usually because we can look at other people's troubles from different angle. Often outside the box.

It's much harder for us to find a resolution to our own problems because we are actually in it and find it difficult to seeing things from a different perspective. We can't see the wood for the trees as the saying goes.

But there is a solution.

It's about finding a way to step out of your current zone so that you can see things more rationally and objectively.

The best way to do this is to write a letter to yourself.

Post it to yourself, then read it when it comes back to you. It will feel like someone else wrote it, and you will be amazed at how you will see things from a completely different angle.

You can even post the reply back to yourself if you want to make it more fun and more interesting.

If you decide to do this, remember to keep your reply positive and do it as if you are helping a dear friend. Which of course you actually are!

So go ahead, and spend a full evening writing a nice honest and frank letter to your best friend (you) then pop it in an envelope with your name and address on the front and stick a first class stamp on it.

Then when it arrives through your letterbox, spend another evening carefully and lovingly writing your reply and post it back to yourself. You will be amazed when you read it.

Dear Brian,

I wonder if it would be OK for me to ask you for a leg up! – It's just that things seem to be a bit shit for me recently. I feel am pretty shit at everything and my life stinks.

My health is in bit, I am eating shite all the time and I really don't like myself any more.

The things I used to enjoy seem to be boring now and nothing seems to buzz me up any more…

Got the idea? – go for it, it can be very enlightening!

LEARN TO SLEEP WELL

Sleeping well directly affects your mental and physical health. Fall short and it can take a serious toll on your daytime energy, productivity, emotional balance, and even your weight. Yet many of us regularly toss and turn at night, struggling to get the sleep we need. Getting a good night's sleep may seem like an impossible goal when you're wide awake at 3 a.m., but you have much more control over the quality of your sleep than you probably realise. Just as the way you feel during your waking hours often hinges on how well you sleep at night, so the cure for sleep difficulties can often be found in your daily routine.

Unhealthy daytime habits and lifestyle choices can leave you tossing and turning at night and adversely affect your mood, brain and heart health, immune system, creativity, vitality, and weight. But by experimenting with the following tips, you can enjoy better sleep at night, boost your health, and improve how you think and feel during the day.

Tip 1: Get in sync with your body's natural sleep cycle

Getting in sync with your body's natural sleep-wake cycle, or circadian rhythm, is one of the most important strategies for sleeping better. If you keep a regular sleep-wake schedule, you'll feel much more refreshed and energized than if you sleep the same number of hours at different times, even if you only alter your sleep schedule by an hour or two.

Try to go to sleep and get up at the same time every day. This helps set your body's internal clock and optimize the quality of your sleep. Choose a bed time when you normally feel tired, so that you don't toss and turn. If you're getting enough sleep, you should wake up naturally without an alarm. If you need an alarm clock, you may need an earlier bedtime.

Avoid sleeping in, even on weekends. The more your weekend/weekday sleep schedules differ, the worse the jetlag like symptoms you'll experience. If you need to make up for a late night, opt for a daytime nap rather than sleeping in. This allows you to pay off your sleep debt without disturbing your natural sleep-wake rhythm.

Be smart about napping. While napping is a good way to make up for lost sleep, if you have trouble falling asleep or staying asleep at night, napping can make things worse. Limit naps to 15 to 20 minutes in the early afternoon.

Fight after-dinner drowsiness. If you get sleepy way before your bedtime, get off the couch and do something mildly stimulating, such as washing the dishes, calling a friend, or getting clothes ready for the next day. If you give in to the drowsiness, you may wake up later in the night and have trouble getting back to sleep.

Tip 2: Control your exposure to light

Melatonin is a naturally occurring hormone controlled by light exposure that helps regulate your sleep-wake cycle. Your brain secretes more melatonin when it's dark, making you sleepy, and less when it's light, making you more alert. However, many aspects of modern life can alter your body's production of melatonin and shift your circadian rhythm.

How to influence your exposure to light during the day:

Expose yourself to bright sunlight in the morning. The closer to the time you get up, the better. Have your coffee outside, for example, or eat breakfast by a sunny window. The light on your face will help you wake up.

Spend more time outside during daylight. Take your work breaks outside in sunlight, exercise outside, or walk your dog during the day instead of at night.

Let as much natural light into your home or workspace as possible. Keep curtains and blinds open during the day, and try to move your desk closer to the window.

If necessary, use a light therapy box. This simulates sunshine and can be especially useful during short winter days.

At night:

Avoid bright screens within 1-2 hours of your bedtime. The blue light emitted by your phone, tablet, computer, or TV is especially disruptive. You can minimize the impact by using devices with smaller screens, turning the brightness down.

Say no to late-night television. Not only does the light from a TV suppress melatonin, but many programs are stimulating rather than relaxing. Try listening to music or audio books instead.

Don't read with backlit devices. Tablets that are backlit are more disruptive than e-readers that don't have their own light source.

When it's time to sleep, make sure the room is dark. Use heavy curtains or shades to block light from windows, or try a sleep mask. Also consider covering up electronics that emit light.

Keep the lights down if you get up during the night. If you need some light to move around safely, try installing a dim nightlight in the hall or bathroom or using a small flashlight. This will make it easier for you to fall back to sleep.

Tip 3: Exercise during the day

People who exercise regularly sleep better at night and feel less sleepy during the day. Regular exercise also improves the symptoms of insomnia and sleep apnea and increases the amount of time you spend in the deep, restorative stages of sleep.

The more vigorously you exercise, the more powerful the sleep benefits. But even light exercise such as walking for just 10 minutes a day improves sleep quality.

Tip 4: Be smart about what you eat and drink

Your daytime eating habits play a role in how well you sleep, especially in the hours before bedtime.

Limit caffeine and nicotine. You might be surprised to know that caffeine can cause sleep problems up to ten to twelve hours after drinking it! Similarly, smoking is another stimulant that can disrupt your sleep, especially if you smoke close to bedtime.

Avoid big meals at night. Try to make dinnertime earlier in the evening, and avoid heavy, rich foods within two hours of bed. Spicy or acidic foods can cause stomach trouble and heartburn.

Avoid alcohol before bed. While a nightcap may help you relax, it interferes with your sleep cycle once you're out.
Avoid drinking too many liquids in the evening. Drinking lots of fluids may result in frequent bathroom trips throughout the night.

Tip 5: Wind down and clear your head

Do you often find yourself unable to get to sleep or regularly waking up night after night? Residual stress, worry, and anger from your day can make it very difficult to sleep well.

Taking steps to manage your overall stress levels and learning how to curb the worry habit can make it easier to unwind at night. You can also try developing a relaxing bedtime ritual to help you prepare your mind for sleep, such as practicing a relaxation technique, taking a warm bath, or dimming the lights and listening to soft music or an audiobook. Also the Tapping (EFT) routine in this book will help too.

A deep breathing exercise to help you sleep

Breathing from your belly rather than your chest can activate the relaxation response and lower your heart rate, blood pressure, and stress levels to help you drift off to sleep.

Lay down in bed and close your eyes.

Put one hand on your chest and the other on your stomach.

Breathe in through your nose. The hand on your stomach should rise. The hand on your chest should move very little.

Exhale through your mouth, pushing out as much air as you can while contracting your abdominal muscles. The hand on your stomach should move in as you exhale, but your other hand should move very little.

Continue to breathe in through your nose and out through your mouth. Try to inhale enough so that your lower abdomen rises and falls. Count slowly as you exhale.

A body scan exercise to help you sleep

By focusing your attention on different parts of your body, you can identify where you're holding any stress or tension, and release it.

Lie on your back, legs uncrossed, arms relaxed at your sides, eyes closed. Focus on your breathing for about two minutes until you start to feel relaxed.

Turn your focus to the toes of your right foot. Notice any tension while continuing to also focus on your breathing. Imagine each deep breath flowing to your toes. Remain focused on this area for at least three to five seconds.

Move your focus to the sole of your right foot. Tune in to any sensations you feel in that part of your body and imagine each breath flowing from the sole of your foot.

Then move your focus to your right ankle and repeat. Move to your calf, knee, thigh, hip, and then repeat the sequence for your left leg. From there, move up your torso, through your lower back and abdomen, your upper back and chest, and your shoulders. Pay close attention to any area of the body that feels tense.

After completing the body scan, relax, noting how your body feels. You should feel so relaxed you can easily fall asleep.

Tip 6: Improve your sleep environment

A peaceful bedtime routine sends a powerful signal to your brain that it's time to wind down and let go of the day's stresses. Sometimes even small changes to your environment can make a big difference to your quality of sleep.

Keep your room dark, cool, and quiet.

Keep noise down. If you can't avoid or eliminate noise from neighbours, traffic, or other people in your household, try masking it with a fan or sound machine. Earplugs may also help.

Keep your room cool. Most people sleep best in a slightly cool room (around 65° F or 18° C) with adequate ventilation. A bedroom that is too hot or too cold can interfere with quality sleep.

Make sure your bed is comfortable. Your bed covers should leave you enough room to stretch and turn comfortably without becoming tangled. If you often wake up with a sore back or an aching neck, you may need to experiment with different levels of mattress firmness, foam toppers, and pillows that provide more or less support.

Reserve your bed for sleeping and sex. By not working, watching TV, or using your phone, tablet, or computer in bed, your brain will associate the bedroom with just sleep and sex, which makes it easier to wind down at night.

Tip 7: Learn ways to get back to sleep

It's normal to wake briefly during the night but if you're having trouble falling back asleep, these tips may help:

Stay out of your head. Hard as it may be, try not to stress over your inability to fall asleep again, because that stress only encourages your body to stay awake. To stay out of your head, focus on the feelings in your body or practice breathing exercises. Take a breath in, then breathe out slowly while saying or thinking the word, "Ahhh." Take another breath and repeat.

Make relaxation your goal, not sleep. If you find it hard to fall back asleep, try a relaxation technique such as visualisation, progressive muscle relaxation, or meditation, which can be done without even getting out of bed. Even though it's not a replacement for sleep, relaxation can still help rejuvenate your body. Take yourself on a pleasant journey back in time.

Do a quiet, non-stimulating activity. If you've been awake for more than 15 minutes, get out of bed and do a quiet, non-stimulating activity, such as reading a book. Keep the lights dim and avoid screens so as not to cue your body that it's time to wake up.

SOLITUDE

I used to have a massive fear of being alone. Believing that the road to happiness was to have a loving partner in my life and lots of friends, and doing stuff together.

A moment of liberation came to me on the day that I found the courage to book a fortnight's holiday to Tenerife. Alone.

After I booked it, I was dreading it. But just because I had paid for it I decided to go.

Well, that holiday was one of the best holidays ever. Just myself to please and consider. A life changing moment.

Now I do not have any fear of being alone so no more desperation to be with someone.

Find a way to spend time alone, maybe a day at the seaside or in the countryside. Make it your habitual monthly treat. It's a fantastic way to 'fathom things out' and just have yourself to please and consider.

Book a holiday – Alone? Where would you like to go?

By the way, you DO NOT need anyone else in your life to become 'whole', you are already whole!

RELATIONSHIPS

In my view, ALL relationships should be easy. Whoever said that successful relationships need working on never had a proper relationship. Relationships should always be easy and flow naturally. OK it's inevitable that you will fall out, disagree and have almighty rows at times. That's normal. But a good healthy meaningful relationship with friends, family or romantic partner should never require hard work!

If your relationships are hard work, exhausting, draining, demanding or even scary, then you are in a toxic kind of relationship. By choice of course!

Some people who badly want love but can't find it, it's full of drama and sorrow and pain. Real love is quiet and patient, but powerful and strong and has no pain. Real love is like waves breaking on the beach. It comes from nowhere, and gathers speed, it has amazing strength and beauty and its regularity grows to be comforting. Just like the waves breaking, its everlasting and always refreshing. But if you get in at the wrong time and out of your depth you could drown!

Watch out for narcissist's and gas lighters. (Google it)

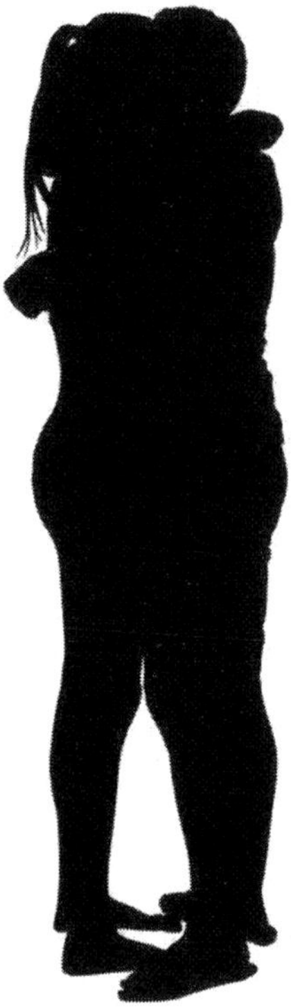

When you fall in love, it is a temporary madness. It erupts like an earthquake then it subsides.

And when it subsides you have to make a decision; you have to work out whether your roots have become so entwined together that it is inconceivable that you two should ever part, because this is what love is.

Love is not breathlessness; it is not excitement, it is not the desire to mate every second of the day, it's not lying awake at night imagining that he is kissing every part of your body.

No, that is just being in love, which any of us can convince ourselves we are. Love, itself, is what is left over when being in love has burned away. Doesn't sound very exciting does it? But, it is.

What do you think ?

IDENTIFYING TOXIC PEOPLE

They are controlling.

They want everything their way and the only agenda they care about is their own. They refuse to take 'no' for an answer unless they are manipulating you or it will ultimately suit their intentions.

They are never wrong

Even if you produce evidence to the contrary, they will never admit to being wrong. Don't expect an apology from them, their enormous ego would never even consider that possibility.

They will drain you

You feel exhausted and depleted just by being in their presence. They are like emotional vampires and they suck he life force right out of you.

They are deceptive

They often come in the guise of being helpful and caring. They may actually be helpful in some ways. But don't be fooled, it always comes with a price tag, or they get some narcissistic pleasure from it. They love having their egos stroked and being told how wonderful they are. Meanwhile, if you do just one thing that they don't like, they will burry you in an instant, without as much as a second thought.

They are liars.

They are the most deceptive people you will ever meet. Everything they do and everything they are is set up to deceive and feed their ego.

They are delusional.

They really believe their own lies. They think they are wonderful. They have an amazing innate ability to fool people, including themselves.

They are impressive.

Distant observers think they are amazing kind considerate nice people. Just a smoke screen set up to make it look like its' you who is the problem.

Remember that you are in the driving seat now. You have a choice as to whether you want to put up with this or not. If you do put up with it, you can only blame yourself.

On you can change this situation.

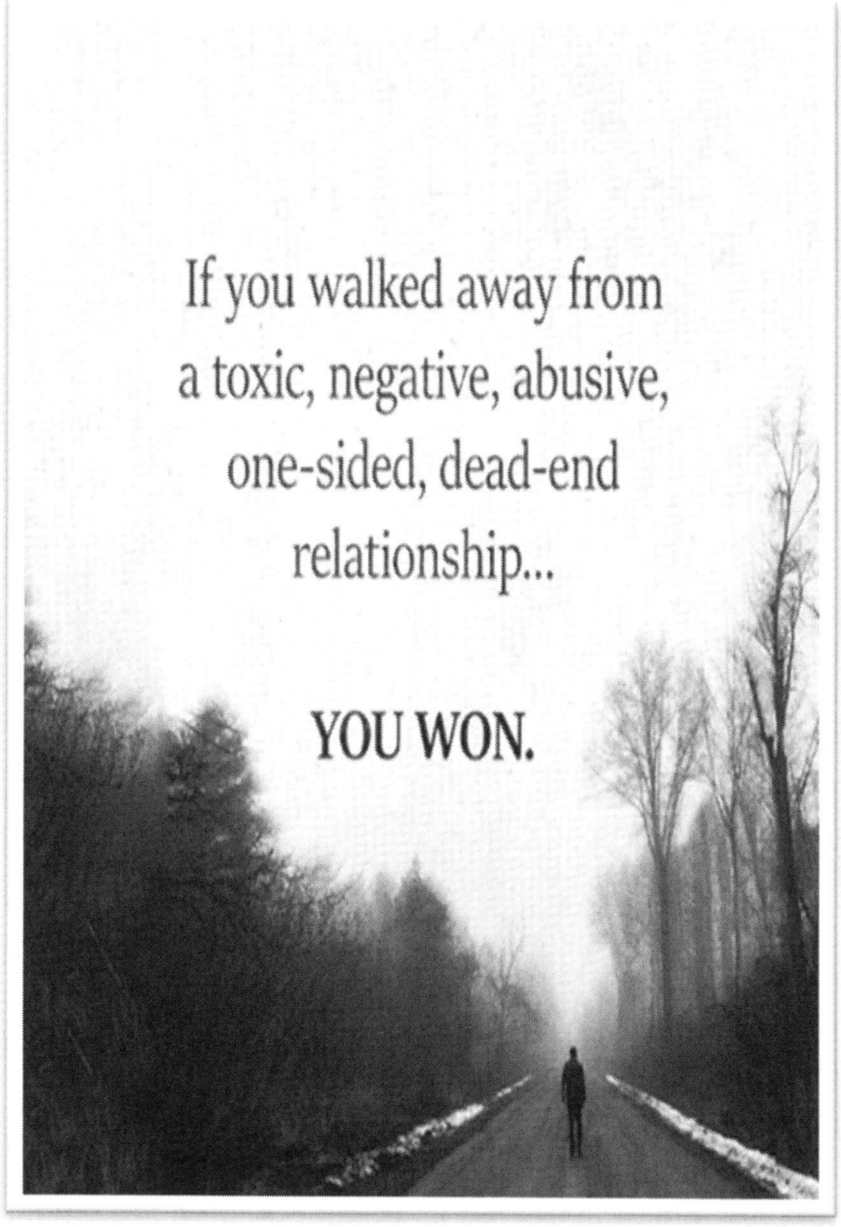
If you walked away from
a toxic, negative, abusive,
one-sided, dead-end
relationship...
YOU WON.

ALTRUISM

A true and honest altruistic way of life will enable ego control and bring a very strong feeling of moral satisfaction.

Benefits of altruism

- Helping others feels good.
- It creates a sense of belonging and reduces isolation.
- It helps keep things in perspective.
- It creates and feeds gratitude.
- It helps make the world a better place, it's contagious!
- The more you do for others, the more you do for yourself.
- Your self esteem and self confidence will rocket sky high
- You will develop a sense of purpose.

Giving is only valid if you give totally unconditional. If you do me a favour, and expect a favour in return, it’s not really giving, it’s a business deal!

If I buy you a pint, don’t tell me you will buy me one back; if you help someone out, don’t be sad when you find the person does not reciprocate that in the future.

Here's something we see and hear often.

"Don't give beggars any money they will just buy drugs or booze with it."

What the actual fuck, that's not giving, that's control. If I was to slip you a tenner, I have no right to tell you how to spend it. And so what if they 'CHOOSE' to buy booze or drugs – Most people I know spend money on their drug of choice!

Oh and when you give that fiver to that beggar, don't plaster it all over FaceBook. That's ego!

There is something powerful and magical when you find a way to give altruistically, whether it's giving your heart, a fiver or a few words of wisdom. Have a go, but remember that true altruism must never be driven by ego.

HAPPINESS

How often have you said, “I just want to be happy”?

How often have you said to someone else, “I just want you to be happy”?

Have you ever stopped to consider exactly what happiness means? What, exactly, is this happiness you are wishing for?

It matters because it’s hard for your wishes for happiness to come true if you aren’t clear about exactly what happiness is.

What is Happiness? A Definition of Happiness

Possibly the best place to start defining happiness is by defining what it is not.

Many people believe that happiness is having fun at a party, the excitement of new experiences, the thrill and passion of sex, or the delights of a fine meal, or a good old drunken night out. These are all wonderful experiences to be cherished and cultivated but they are not happiness.

These experiences are the definition of **pleasure**. They are experiences to have and let pass. A meal to savour, then digest. A party to enjoy then let wind down. The passion to enjoy and the warm afterglow to linger in.

Pleasure is fleeting and must be if it is to continue to please us because if we have these joyful experiences all the time, our brains adapt and turn pleasure into routine. Once that happens, it takes even more to make us feel good again. Chasing pleasure is not happiness.

So, if happiness is not the same thing as pleasure, then what is happiness?

Happiness comes when you feel satisfied and fulfilled. Happiness is a feeling of contentment that life is just as it should be. Perfect happiness, enlightenment, comes when you have all of your needs satisfied.

While the perfect happiness of enlightenment may be hard to achieve, and even harder to maintain, happiness is not an either/or case. There are nearly limitless degrees of happiness between the bliss of enlightenment and the despair of depression. Most of us fall somewhere between, closer to the middle than the edges.

Maybe it would be acceptable to be happy 70% of the time and sad 30% of the time. Most people I know have it the other way round and find they can't separate the feeling of happiness from pleasure.

Can you?

TEN WAYS TO FEEL HAPPY

Go on, practice them all.

DARE TO FAIL

As a child, some people were ridiculed and even punished if they failed certain tasks. This in turn made those people feel bad, unworthy and useless. The feelings evoked during that time can be firmly embedded in our subconscious mind leaving us with massive fears of failure and holding us back from so many amazing opportunities.

Reflect back in time when your baby first learned to walk. The baby took those first three steps and fell over hurting their knees and triggering lots of tears. But with a little encouragement, they stand up again and have another go, only to fall again and create more pain on top of those wounds on the knees. Then they get up and have another go, and another go, then eventually mastering there newly learned technique for mobility. This would indicate that we are born with a desire to succeed.

Now, imagine the same scenario as an adult, you would probably take those first three steps, fall over, feel the pain and say 'fek that, I won't do that again!'

The baby is naturally programmed to keep on trying until they succeed and become successful. But as they grow older, this wonderful natural instinct is replaced with humiliation, ridicule and sometimes even punishment for failure.

So due to our childhood experiences of failure, we now have a fear of failure as an adult which inevitably restricts our chances of becoming successful at anything we attempt to do. In some cases to the degree that we don't even attempt to do anything! We have no skills, no drive, no direction and no life purpose.

Successful people have a completely different perception to failure. They actually embrace it!

We often hear from successful people that failure is an inevitable stepping stone on the way to accomplishing our goals.

But how many failures does it take to reach success?

Well, for the Rocket Chemical Company, now known as the WD-40 Company, the answer was 39.

In 1953, founder Norm Larsen's three-man staff set out to create a water displacement formula to be used as a rust-prevention solvent and degreaser in the aerospace industry.
After 39 unsuccessful attempts, the San Diego-based business perfected the formula. The name of the product, WD-40, reflects its history: "Water Displacement perfected on the 40th try."
Thomas Edison was accused of failing to make a light bulb work after over one thousand attempts. His view was

that he was give one thousand opportunities to learn! I for one, am glad that he never gave up!

Successful people it seems, have a completely different perception to failure. They welcome it, they embrace it and they actually have 'nice' feelings evoked by failure.

So, maybe you could forgive those who initially installed those horrible feelings around failure. They probably never meant to hurt you anyway, their intentions were probably good. And then you have a wonderful opportunity to change your perception and feelings towards failure by seeing failure as an amazing and exciting opportunity to learn something new.

Go on – dare to fail!

SUCCESSFUL PEOPLE FALL OVER

Here is a look at the things which our own mind can sometimes do to throw a spanner into the works for some reason or another. We are often completely unaware that we are doing this and as a result may well be certain that the blame for our failure rests elsewhere. And there we may have a serious problem, for if the problem is not where we keep on trying to look for it, how on earth will we ever find it and deal with it sufficiently to overcome it?

By far the most common, most obvious, and definitely most counter-productive of these hidden negativities is giving up at the first opportunity. At the first sign of the tiniest thing going wrong, you are off, proclaiming that the whole idea was nonsensical, that you should never have believed this positive thinking rubbish, now you're going to have start all over again, you should have known better... etc. And then you're nicely off the hook until next time, when you'll be able to lay the blame squarely at somebody else's doorstep.

Nobody ever became successful without tripping up somewhere along the way. You **WILL**, undoubtedly, have things go wrong, like any successful person. Successful people are those who overcome their obstacles one-by-one until they get to where they wanted to go; the 'quick' scheme for instant success is nothing more than a myth, or EVERYONE would be doing it! The only way to achieve lasting success is to build it yourself and build it well.

You have to keep sight of your goal and remember that the longest journey starts with just one small step. Yes, yes, I know that you've probably heard that old Oriental cliché before and you're probably as tired of it and as unimpressed by it as I am. Well, I've used it because I like to add something. The longest journey might well start with just one small step, but it is truly important that all the steps that follow it go in the same direction! There, that's better.

If you keep on changing direction every time something doesn't go exactly the way you planned it to, you'll run around like a headless chicken forever, never reaching any goal, never getting anywhere in particular, and never really knowing where you are or what you are doing. You'll have joined that great band of "will-be-one-day's" who are always going to make it next week, or next year... or in their next life, maybe.

STICKING WITH IT

One of the positive affirmations I give my consulting room clients with a history of this sort of behaviour is: I have the courage and tenacity to stay with an idea I believe in, because if I believe in it, I can make it work. The word 'courage' is used advisedly, because you do need it to stick with your plans from time to time, especially at the beginning. But avoiding failure by 'copping out' is not exactly what you would call success, is it? It's not the way to gain respect - your own for yourself, or anybody else's - and you deserve better. So stick with it for long enough for your plans to bear fruit and solve those 'running-in' problems as they arise. Your confidence in yourself and your belief in your abilities - two VITAL components of success - will increase with each problem you solve, with each obstacle you overcome.

Remember that rule: Do the same thing in the same way and you'll get the same result. When something doesn't work as you want it to, change something; anything - just do something differently; because if what you did last time didn't work, then it's probably not going to work this time either.

WHOSE FAULT IS IT ANYWAY?

Maybe you have had the experience of failing in the past and this makes it difficult for you to maintain self-belief; well, you were less experienced then and you had not had the benefit of the teachings of this book. Besides which, the past cannot actually exert any influence on the future; only an individual's reaction to it can do that. It's worth remembering, too, that failure is not the end - unless you give up.

So where you have got memories of lack of success from the past, make an effort to find out where you went wrong - because you did, somewhere along the line, if only because you did not solve the problems that caused you to fail. Of course, it is much easier to blame other people, circumstances, lack of finance, unfair competition, lack of support from your family, staffing problems, recession, media mistakes with your advertising, problems with suppliers, your bankers, the weather, next door's cat... and so on. Any of these circumstances may have been partly to blame, but a successful individual will have to deal with all of them from time to time (except, maybe, for next door's cat!). An acquaintance of mine once said: "You know when something goes wrong and I discover it's my fault, I breathe a sigh of relief, because I can get control of that. I hate things that are completely out of my control - but then I can't remember when I last found one of those!"

We all know that you are supposed to learn from your mistakes. Now, how on earth can you do that if you are never prepared to admit you are wrong? In order to learn from mistakes you must first admit that you made the mistake - or you will never be able to admit that you learned anything from it, even to yourself. And if you cannot admit you have learned something then the chances are that you'll make that self-same mistake again, sooner or later. Or one very much like it anyway.

NOBODY ELSE EXPECTS YOU TO BE PERFECT, SO NEITHER SHOULD YOU.

How do you feel about other people who claim never to put a foot wrong, dismissing all their mistakes as being someone else's fault? I'll bet you've got more respect for the person who can see where he made a mistake and then turn that knowledge to an advantage next time around!

THERE'S MORE!

Some of the best lessons we ever learn are learned from our mistakes and failures. The errors of the past are the success and wisdom of our future.

If we make our goal to live a life of compassion and unconditional love, then the world will indeed become a garden where all kinds of flowers can bloom and grow.

One forgives as much as one loves.

Learn to get in touch with the silence within yourself and know that everything in this life has a purpose. Live every day as if it was your last because the future belongs to those who believe in the beauty of their dreams!

Take time to notice and appreciate the tiny miracles around you, and feel content in the now!

Accept that you cannot change another person, let others be who they are and simply love who you are! It is not up to you to take responsibility for others!

If you can make even a small difference to someone's life, you'll start making a difference to your own life too. We are all part of a wonderful journey!

When you get into a tight place and everything goes against you, till it seems as though you could not hang on a minute longer, never give up, for that is just the place and time that the tide will turn!

Even a mistake may turn out to be the one thing necessary to a worthwhile achievement!

Remember that whatever feelings you have within you are attracting your tomorrow.

Worry attracts more worry. Anxiety attracts more anxiety. Unhappiness attracts more unhappiness. Dissatisfaction attracts more dissatisfaction.

And...

Joy attracts more joy. Happiness attracts more happiness. Peace attracts more peace. Gratitude attracts more gratitude. Kindness attracts more kindness. Love attracts more love.

Your job is an inside one. To change your world, all you have to do is change the way you think.

How easy is that?

(Whatever your answer is, you are right)

YOU HAVE A RIGHT TO BE YOU

Being YOU is the only way to truly live.

You must be what it is that you're seeking. In this universe of attraction and energy, you can't have a desire to attract a mate who's confident, generous, non-judgmental, and gentle, and expect that desire to be manifested if you're thinking and acting in non-confident, selfish, judgmental, or arrogant ways.

Spend time with nice people who are smart, driven, kind, caring, considerate, compassionate and like-minded. Choose friends who you are proud to know, people you admire, who love and respect you, people who make your day a little brighter simply by being in it.

Relationships should help you, not hurt you.

Surround yourself with people who reflect the person you want to be.

Life is too short to spend time with people who suck the happiness out of you. When you free yourself from negative people, you free yourself to be YOU – and being YOU is the only way to truly live.

Don't live your life with hate in your heart. You will end up hurting yourself more than the people you hate.

Forgiveness is not saying, “What you did to me is okay.” It is saying, “I’m not going to let what you did to me ruin my happiness anymore.”

Forgiveness is the remedy. It doesn’t mean you’re erasing the past, or forgetting what happened. It means you’re letting go of the resentment and pain, and choosing to learn from the incident and move on with your life.

Remember, the less time you spend hating the people who hurt you, the more time you’ll have to love the people who love you.

Whatever happens, everything will be OK in the end. And if it’s not OK it’s not the end!

Wishing you love, peace and continued happiness.

Keep on keeping on!

WHEN

So, now you are almost at the end of this book and the rest is down to you. It's your responsibility to look after yourself and make the necessary changes to claim your birth right to be happy.

So when will you do this?

- After Christmas?
- After the kids leave school?
- After the exams?
- After your mother passes away?
- After coronation street?
- After you lose weight?
- After the operation?
- Or maybe you could wait until the tortoise crosses the road.

If you are really serious about making changes, why wait?

I am not suggesting that you pack your bags, leave your children and sail off to Jamaica, but maybe you could start to make small changes on a daily basis rather than continually finding a reason not to make the changes.

Most people know what they should be doing, but they keep on finding a way to put it off. Well, the sooner you start, the sooner the new you will evolve and the sooner you get to claim your birth right to be happy.

ACKNOWLEDGEMENT

Heartfelt thanks to my friend and colleague Charlotte Redfearn for her kind words in the forward section of this book.

Also thanking my own personal proof reader, Yvette Botterill for a splendid job well done and in a very short space of time.

Special thanks to my kinesiologist, Michelle. She made me so miserable and then it all changed!

Thanks to the nice bloke in India who did the illustration of me on the front cover. Fabulous job. Courtesy of Fiver.com

And of course acknowledging my thanks and gratitude to you for taking the time to read this book and hopefully becoming part of my million!

If you would like to comment on the content of this book or feedback any positive changes that you made after reading it, you are welcome to contact me on my personal email address. bg@innervisionsuk.com I would love to hear from you.

If you enjoyed the book, please log in to your Amazon account and submit a review. Thanks.

DISCLAIMER

This book and its content does not provide medical advice and is not a substitute for medical advice or intervention.

The content is for informational purposes only. Consult with your doctor (GP) on all medical issues regarding your condition and its treatment.

The content is not intended to be a substitute for professional medical advice, diagnosis, or treatment. It is not a substitute for a medical examination, nor does it replace the need for services provided by a medical professional.

Always seek the advice of your medical professional before making any changes to your treatment. Any medical questions should be directed to your personal doctor.

Brian Glenn (the book author) makes no warranties, either expressed or implied concerning the accuracy, applicability, reliability or suitability of the contents of this book.

Brian Glenn (the book author) shall in no event be held liable for any direct, indirect incidental or other consequential damages arising directly or indirectly from any use of the information contained in this book.

All content is for information only and is not warranted for content accuracy or any other implied or explicit purpose.

INNERVISIONS SCHOOL OF CLINICAL HYPNOSIS

Established in 1996, Innervisions School of Clinical Hypnosis is the training provider of choice providing specialised training in modern clinical hypnosis. And with over 25 years of training experience behind us, we are now one of the UK's leading training providers.

We aim to be the best in our particular field and to surpass our student's expectations; our teaching methods are unique, supportive, warm and friendly. We are dedicated to this profession and we intend to assist and train each and every student to become a competent practitioner in modern clinical hypnosis and hypnotherapy.

The course is designed to be of particular relevance to those in the caring profession as well as anyone who has an interest in the field of human potential and personal development. Whilst academic qualifications may be an advantage, we regard it as only being a small part of the learning curve to becoming a competent clinical hypnotherapist.

This hypnotherapy training course is therefore open to those with a genuine interest in hypnotherapy irrespective of race, religion, and environmental classification, even though they may not have any relevant prior learning or training.

A UNIQUE OPPORTUNITY TO TRAIN FOR A REWARDING NEW CAREER

For two exciting days, Discover Hypnotherapy with our world class tutors and find out if hypnotherapy is the right career for you. You are invited to apply for a FREE place on our foundation weekend. Absolutely 100% free and unconditional.

www.innervisions.co.uk

ACCREDITATION

Our hypnotherapy training courses are fully supported and accredited by the General Hypnotherapy Standards Council.

Our practitioner level training course has been assessed and validated at practitioner level by The General Hypnotherapy Standards Council (UK). Graduates are eligible for professional registration with The General Hypnotherapy Register at full practitioner status.

GHSC

General Hypnotherapy Standards Council

Accredited Training

The GHSC was a key participant within the Working Group for Hypnotherapy Regulation whose primary purpose was to facilitate agreed standards within the profession and to subsequently bring about Voluntary Self-regulation (VSR), an officially recognised status, for the entire industry.

To facilitate this, the Group actively co-operated with other industry representatives within the Hypnotherapy Regulatory Forum (a body established by the now defunct Prince's Foundation for Integrated Health) and as a consequence VSR was finally established via the Natural Healthcare Council (CNHC) set up in 2008 with Department of Health funding - when it admitted Hypnotherapy into its regulatory system on 1st December 2010.

CNHC

Complementary & Natural Healthcare Council

DIPLOMA

Our Diploma in Hypnotherapy and Psychotherapy has been validated by the General Hypnotherapy Standards Council (GHSC) and Graduates from this course are eligible for professional registration with the General Hypnotherapy Register (the GHSC's registering agency) at full Practitioner status, together with the acquisition of the industry based award - the General Qualification in Hypnotherapy Practice (GQHP).

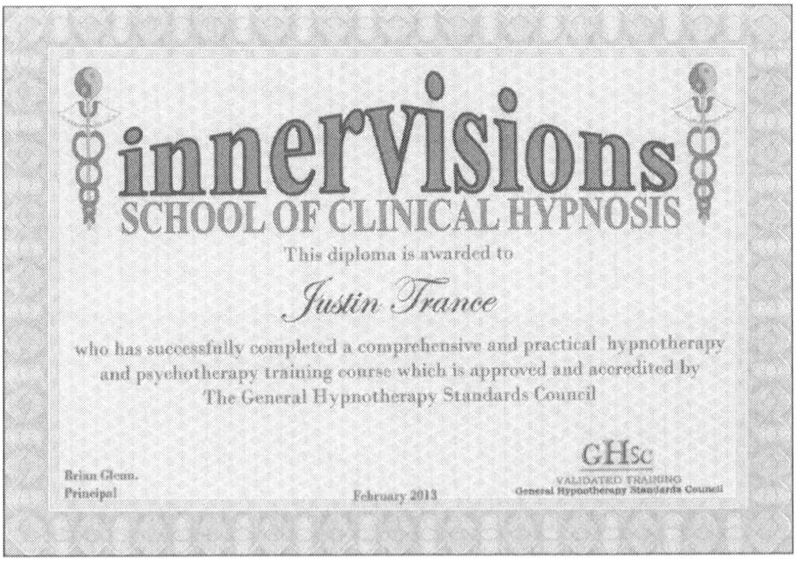

Graduates of this course will also be eligible to register with the Complementary and Natural Healthcare Council (CNHC). For more information visit **www.cnhc.org.uk**

Whatever feelings you have within you are attracting your tomorrow.

Worry attracts more worry. Anxiety attracts more anxiety. Unhappiness attracts more unhappiness. Dissatisfaction attracts more dissatisfaction.

And . . .

Joy attracts more joy. Happiness attracts more happiness. Peace attracts more peace. Gratitude attracts more gratitude. Kindness attracts more kindness. Love attracts more love.

Your job is an inside one. To change your world, all you have to do is change the way you feel inside.

And now you know how to!

Printed in Great Britain
by Amazon

44410417R00059